The New Kid on the Team

Written by John Lockyer
Illustrated by Raymond McGrath

Our team had never won a game. One day, before a game, a new boy joined the team. Our coach told us his name, but no one remembered it, so we called him the new kid.

The new kid was smaller than us, but he
had knobbly knees, big hands, wide feet and
sharp eyes. He had an old, worn-out glove
and his own bat. He wore baggy shorts and
a floppy hat that covered most of his face.

Before each game, our team always warmed up. The new kid showed us he could play in any position — pitcher, catcher, fielder and batter.

We hit balls at him — high balls, low balls,
fast balls and slow balls — and he didn't
drop one. No one ran faster or threw the
ball harder than the new kid. The new kid
was just what our team needed.

We were playing the Cobras that day. The Cobras aren't a nice team. The last time we played them, we lost 3-nil. They called us losers.

But this time we didn't play like losers. It was a tight game. We stopped the Cobras getting any runs, but we didn't get any runs either. We played well, but the new kid played the best. He was really good at fielding and batting. He never gave up. He made us all try harder.

We were in the last innings. We were batting. We had two batters out and the new kid was our last batter. Everyone but the new kid said the game would end in a draw.

The umpire pulled his mask over his face and said, "Batter up!"

The new kid stepped up to the batter's box. He did a couple of knee bends. He swung the bat round and round his head. He set his feet wide. He lifted the bat above his shoulder. He leaned forward and stood as still as a post. He gave the pitcher a cold, hard look.

The umpire leaned forward, too, and said, "Play ball!"

The pitcher swung his arm and let the ball go. It was a good pitch. The ball flew fast and straight.

The new kid watched the ball dip, then he moved forward and swung the bat. He cracked the ball hard. It zipped over the pitcher's head. It flew high and wide and far out into the field. A fielder rushed to grab it. The new kid dropped the bat. He put his head down and ran. He raced towards base one.

"Go!" we shouted. **"Go! Go! Go!"**

Dust whirled behind the new kid.

"He's on base one!" we shouted.

11

The fielder had the ball.

"He's on base two!" we shouted.

The fielder threw the ball, but it was a bad throw.

"He's on base three!" we shouted.

The short stop had the ball. He threw it to the catcher, but it wasn't even close. The new kid skidded into home base and the ball rolled in behind him.

The new kid had hit a home run.

We jumped off our seats. We cheered. We whistled. We clapped. We leaped up and down. We'd won the game!

We ran on to the field. We grabbed the new kid. We shook his hand. We hugged him. We slapped him on the back. We lifted him up on our shoulders. Someone knocked off his hat. Two thick, black plaits fell down the new kid's back. The plaits had ribbons dangling from the ends.

Everyone went quiet. We put the new kid back on the ground.

The new kid looked at us and grinned. "Do you want me to play next week?" she asked.

We looked at the new kid, then we looked at each other and laughed. "Oh, yes!" we shouted.

"Yes! Yes! Yes! We want you to play every game!"

The New Kid on the Team is a Recount.

A **recount** tells . . .

- **who** the story is about (the characters)
- **when** the story happened
- **where** the story is set.

Who	Where	When
		⊙ne day, before the game.

A recount tells what happens.

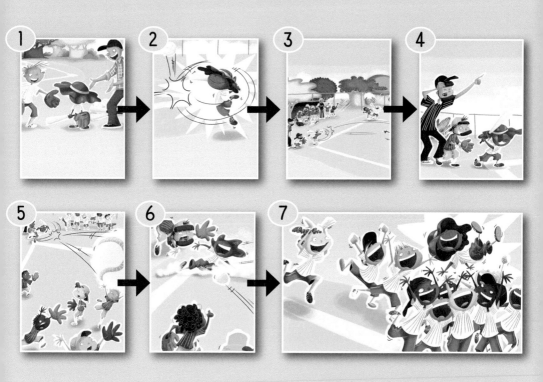

A recount has a conclusion.

Guide Notes

Title: The New Kid on the Team
Stage: Fluency

Text Form: Recount
Approach: Guided Reading
Processes: Thinking Critically, Exploring Language, Processing Information
Written and Visual Focus: Illustrative Text

THINKING CRITICALLY
(sample questions)
- What do you think this story could be about? Look at the title and discuss.
- Look at the cover. What do you think the kid is doing?
- Look at pages 2 and 3. What kind of sport do you think the team plays?
- Look at pages 4 and 5. Why does a sports team warm up before a game?
- Look at pages 6 and 7. How do you think the new kid made the rest of the team try harder?
- Look at pages 8 and 9. How do you think the new kid feels? Why?
- Look at pages 12 and 13. How do you think the other team feels? Why?
- Look at pages 16 and 17. Why do you think the new kid let the team think she was a boy?

EXPLORING LANGUAGE

Terminology
Title, cover, illustrations, author, illustrator

Vocabulary
Clarify: warmed up, fielder, innings, draw, umpire, pitcher, base one, short stop
Nouns: team, game, glove, bat, plaits
Verbs: swung, lifted, leaned, joined
Focus the students' attention on **homonyms**, **antonyms** and **synonyms** if appropriate.

Print Conventions
Apostrophes – possessive (batter's box, pitcher's head, new kid's back), contraction (didn't, aren't, he's)